Turning your dreams into reality

OVER 50.BIZ

AGE IS NO BARRIER

How everyone over 50 can start their own dream business

By Tom Edge

©2005 By Training Projects All Rights Reserved

©2005 By Training Projects All Rights Reserved
ISBN Numbers: 0-9551161-0-4 & 978-0-9551161-0-0
Published By Tom Edge
6 Himley Crescent Wolverhampton England WV4 - 5DA
Tel: 01902-335507
email:tom@over50.biz
website: www.over50.biz

One copy only for personal use may be reproduced from the website or disk. Please email The Editor, before you reproduce any additional copies of this material. Vigorous legal action will be taken if we find it is being stolen or sold.

Requests for permission or further information should be addressed to the Permission Department, Training Projects 6 Himley Crescent Wolverhampton WV4 5DA. 01902-335507 or email to: tom@over50.biz with "Permission" as subject.

Reproduction or translation of any part of this work beyond that permitted by news reporting or student works without the permission of the copyright owner is unlawful.

All International Copyright Laws Apply. British and International law forbid any commercial use or duplication of this copyright material without prior licensing. This publication is designed to provide accurate and authoritative information in regard to the subject matter presented.

It is sold with the understanding that the publisher is not engaged in rendering legal, accounting, or other licensed professional services.

If legal advice or other expert assistance is required, the services of a competent professional person in your area should be sought.

The term "He" is used throughout this text. This is to aid understanding of the topic and not to imply any preference of gender. "He" should be read as He/She where appropriate.

©2005Cover designed by Tom Edge

Published in England

Table of Contents

Contents	3
Dedication	5
Small Business Perspective	9
The 10 Step Process To Starting A Business	11
The 7 Most Common Errors	13
Seven Suggestions For Avoiding The 2 Year Trap	17
Your Attitude	18
Why Start A Small Business?	20
Women In Business	22
Seven Benchmarks Of Success	23
Which Business?	25
Life Style Businesses	27
SWOT Analyse Yourself	29
Wheel Of Fortune - Problem Solving	30
Market Research and Pricing	35
The Different Types Of Business	42

Insurance and Pensions	48
All About Franchises	50
How To Build A Better Business	54
The Sales & Marketing Machine	58
The Marketing Plan	63
The Finance Machine	66
Internet Businesses	69
The Business Plan	72
Special Considerations For The Over 50s	82
Where To Go For Help	84
101 Final Thoughts	85
Order Form -Tapes & Books	89

Dedication

This book is dedicated to you the reader, may you find happiness and prosperity through applying the tools, tips and techniques in this book.

"Pray for potatoes but pick up a hoe."

The definition of wisdom: "The correct application of knowledge" Knowledge only becomes powerful when you use it. All the knowledge in the world is of little use until you apply it. To put it other ways:

Nothing happens if nothing happens!

If you want a different result you will have to do something different. I found a book 25 years ago that changed my life. "The Lazy Mans Way to Riches" by Joe Karbo was just what I needed when I was considering giving up my business and looking down the situations vacant columns for a "proper job". After applying his ideas to my business it went out of the cul-de-sac and onto the highway. Since this time I've become a bibliophile (bookaholic) and collected over 300 books for my own personal library. None of them has given me the same high as that first one, or has been as useful.

This is simply because I acted upon the first book and only read the other 299....Hence the statement "Pray for potatoes but pick up a hoe" Only action gets things done, so apply the tools tips and techniques outlined in this book and your business dream will soon ecome a reality.

Tom Edge 2005

Preface

By Tom Egelhoff
Director of Marketing - Eagle Marketing Group

When Tom Edge asked me to write the preface to this book on Business Start Up for the older entrepreneur, I had no idea he was actually going to blame me for the whole project. However, while reading the introduction I discovered that he attributed the notion to write a business start-up book to a conversation we had while he visited me in Bozeman Montana in Y2000. While I don't remember having that conversation, and therefore can plausibly deny all responsibility for the end product, I was interested in reading the manuscript.

I can bluntly say, as a marketing professional for over 20 years, that this is the most practical and usable help for people to start a small businesses that I've ever seen. By using dozens of examples and talking in non-technical language, Tom has made the secrets of starting a small business intellectually available to a wide audience. There are many good, practical ideas here, even for people with lots of experience.

As you read through the book, I would encourage you to apply the ideas to your business. While you'll find some outstanding ones that you can apply immediately, the real benefit of the book will come from better understanding the perspective that is needed to successfully operate any small business. As Tom clearly points out, small businesses who rely only on word of mouth without actually promoting their business are applying a dangerous tactic. Most small businesses suffer with "feast and famine" so it is much safer to practice marketing advertising and promoting your business to be ready for the lean times which invariably will come Also information on the availability of help, grants, and a variety of other resources can help guide decisions to help you maximise profits and minimise your risks.

Prior to this book, there has been little in the way of practical guidance. I am very familiar with most of the popular literature on small business start-up and find little of it to be of much use for most of my small business clients, because it is frequently written by academics and none practitioners. Or, as Tom would say, "Many people talk the talk but few of these have walked the walk"

Tom's book does an excellent job of adapting traditional thought and technology to the unique problems of starting a small business. If you're over 50 and thinking of starting a small business there is no better first stop source of information available than here. I intend to distribute this manuscript to clients for whom I provide marketing consulting service. I think you'll find it to be helpful and informative too....

Tom Egelhoff
Director of Marketing
Eagle Marketing Group
Bozeman, Montana
January 2005

Small Business Perspective

Pain and hardship

Over 80% of start up businesses fail within the first two years and a massive 97% fail in the first ten years. Most of these failures and the resulting pain and hardship could be avoided if you, the owner manager, take on board just a few simple ideas outlined in this book.

Get help!
There is a lot of free help out there just for the asking.

The aim of this book is to explain, in the simplest way, how to start up a successful small business if you are over 50 years of age, while avoiding the main reasons for business failure. If you are an older entrepreneur you have experience and wisdom to bring to the venture but you also may have fixed ideas, a low risk culture and the wrong caricature image of an owner/manager.

Balancing is the key to your business

When he decided to be both the Salesman and Production Manager in his fastener business my cousin had serious stress and financial problems. His only mistake was to think his products were so good and so cheap they would sell themselves. They didn't and he went bust.

Businesses can be likened to a three legged stool having a Production leg, a Marketing leg and a Finance leg. You need to be equally good at all three if your business is to keep in balance. You will also need a work/life balance plan if you are to avoid becoming a workaholic.

Most people who start a small business are good at producing the goods or delivering the service. In many cases they have been doing the job for years as a hobby or while working for someone else. Circumstances then get the entrepreneur to go it alone and start their own business.

In the case of the older entrepreneur this is often the result of downsizing or retiring too early, pension not performing, or just spending too much time under your partners feet.

Following his third redundancy Joe, a friend of mine, started a home carpet cleaning business. I asked him if he wanted any help to set it up and he refused saying "How can you help me?" It took him six months of hard work and stress to lose all of his redundancy money.

Meanwhile Keith, a client of mine, came across some lawnmowers while trading on e-bay. He decided to start a gardening business. Following just a few simple marketing ideas he is now earning a good living and only working three days a week.

Whatever your reason for starting a business this book will help you if you can just keep an open mind…

Here is the simple version of starting a business…

2 The 10 Step Process of Starting a Business

1. Selection of Product or Service
Determine growth industries, segment these industries, find a gap in the market. Perform INDEPENDENT tests on these results, ensure consistency of product or raw material supply, make an unemotional decision as to which market gap you will address first.

2. Your Personal Development
Determine the experiences and disciplines your business will need and any gaps you may have. (SWOT Analysis) Determine exactly your personal goals and your business goals <u>and check they are in harmony!</u> Have a personal health check and start your health regime.

3. Your First Office
Choose a quiet, bright place to work. Quiet is all-important. Have a desk and equipment used only for work. Buy used office equipment to start. Use a simple desk management system. Also develop a system for storing promotional materials, letters etc. Develop a simple system to trigger customer call back and follow up. Develop a system to keep your finances straight. Most of these can be done with software but BACK UP REGULARLY and store back ups in another building. Have a Treasure Map, Year Planner and Notice Board on the wall. Have everyone in the house treat this space with reverence.

4. Choose Your Image
Vital to choose a business name and colour scheme appropriate to your product and industry. Have this image run through all of your stationary (see Microsoft.com for "Publisher" templates) Get professionally printed stationary.

5. Begin to turn cash immediately
Start selling immediately to generate cash flow. Develop your marketing image. Get an appropriate web address. Achieve early goals soon to develop a success momentum.

6. Develop your products and services
Make products and services customer driven. Establish patents, trademarks, copyright and other protection. Develop your sales machine and distribution networks.

7. Develop your business plan - and start to follow it.
Develop your sales forecasting for the next 3 years, projected budgets, cash flow, find ways of reducing costs and borrowing cheap money. Make your money work very hard. (Leverage)

8. Attract capital
Give professional mouth watering presentations, conduct yourself professionally and dress appropriately during the negotiations.

9. Set up sales networks
Get on a personal selling skills course. Don't rely only on word of mouth, make all employees sales oriented, set targets, train, motivate, give incentives to your sales people, recognise the best, feed their ego needs, get daily feedback information on each level in the sales process, modify training to fill the gaps.

10. Check your Work/Life balance.
Are you still in line with your personal requirements? Be honest with yourself! How many hours are you "at work" each week? Develop an exit strategy with a specific date. Along with your business goals an exit strategy will focus your efforts.

3 The 7 Most Common Errors

Error 1 - Marketing Basics
"Don't tell customers what you can do - ask them what they want!"
Often the first mistake is to make the business "product led" and not "customer driven". In the short term this is often a success and word of mouth generates a lot of business but without constant improvement people soon go elsewhere.

Error 2 - Pricing
Always charge as much as the market will stand while keeping your costs to a minimum. Many people base their selling price on costs. While it's obvious you must sell products for more than they cost you do not base your selling price on cost. Experiment with your prices - upwards first! My friend's carpet cleaning was low priced but his customers would not buy. They associated cheap with inferior so would not buy his service. Base your prices on what the customer is prepared to pay. Many businesses are delighted when customers start paying a mark up price exceeding five times cost.

Error 3 - Poor Advertising and Promotion
Being too busy the owner/manager does not have the time, or see the need to practice advertising or promotion. After all he now has all the customers he can handle...

However word of mouth advertising eventually stops working. People stop recommending when they find something newer to recommend. And whatever business you are in - the market always always moves.

Your Notes:

Suddenly he has to be come pro-active in advertising and promoting his business. He should have prepared for this long before because if he doesn't have a sales machine already fueled, lubricated and ready to go, by the time he has built one and got it producing sales he is out of business.

I strongly suggest you don't make this error. Invest in Marketing, Advertising and Promotion Books See: www.trainingprojects.com for the best.

Error 5 - Poor Sales Process
Many people have the wrong perception of sales people. I thought they were tacky trying to separate me from my money and give me little in return.

How wrong can you be? Top salespeople care for their customers because they want you to keep coming back. The best ones believe wholeheartedly in their product and are well motivated to tell their story to five or more brand new prospects every day!

Build a sales machine or process. Experiment with it until it works just as well, if not better than your products or services. Give your salespeople the credit they deserve and financial incentives to bring in the business.

Error 6 - Poor Financial Controls
Lack of financial control is another major reason for business failure. Most small businesses don't work to budgets so forget something or don't get paid and run out of money. You need to be able to "see" how your money comes in and goes out before you can control it. This is easily remedied by using a computer with a financial package that gives control information in the form of a picture (pie chart or graph)
Owing tax and not being able to pay has closed more businesses than

anything else. Keep your receipts in date order and invest the taxman's money in a safe, accessible, area of your business where you can retrieve it easily.

Error 7- Poor Recruitment and Leadership

A leader achieves a goal through a team, made up of individuals.
When you hire your first employee you should go on a leadership course. Stop doing work and start managing others to do the work for you; otherwise employees will become problems to manage not assets to help.

7 Tips to Hire the Right person

1 Plan personnel requirements - in line with your organisation chart
2 Attract applicants - tell them your vision
3 Select employees - get them to "buy into" your vision
4 Induct and orient them to your company
          - spend time with them first day!
5 Train them - using your operations manual
6 Motivate them and set goals with them
7 Evaluate their performance

Your notes:

4 Seven Suggestions for Avoiding the 2 Year Trap

1. Visit a Business Support Agency and ask for help.

2. Do your market research before you start and regularly update it afterwards.

3. Have a business plan for the first 3 years. Not just a financial plan but also a marketing plan. Decide to run your accounts on a computer.

4. Before you start, learn as much about business as possible, especially selling and negotiating. Most people will attend courses to upgrade their job skills but few upgrade their business skills. It is your business skills that will make you money and help you survive.

5. Have specific weekly goals and a daily plan how you will achieve them. If you get lost - ask for help. This will save you from running around in circles for the first two years.

6. Even a self-employed person should have an organisation chart showing how the business will look when you have finished building it. The chart will remind you what you are working towards on a daily basis.

7. Have an operating manual so someone else can run your business while you're away. The manual will have tick box statements how to do each task, and a box at the bottom for their signiture. The manual will serve as a training manual for new employees.

Just stay focused on the goal and enjoy the daily journey!

5 Your Attitude

"Your attitude at the start of any venture is the biggest single factor in attaining success"

Attitude is a little thing that makes a BIG difference. When starting your own small business you have to be able to turn your hand to most things and be flexible - you are the boss but you are also the cleaner, secretary, accountant, salesman etc.

Answer the following questions honestly about yourself. Get several people who know you well to answer them, and don't interrupt when they are giving their opinions, remember there is a difference between listening and waiting for your turn to talk.

Can you handle the responsibility of running a business?

Are you reliable?

Are you physically well?

Do you have the right attitude?

Are you punctual?

Do you have any money to put in the business?

Can you cope with long and irregular hours?

Do you have sufficient organisational skills?

Some highly successful business people had none of those attributes when they started their businesses but they were willing to grow towards

attaining them…
Can you take advice?

Asking for help is one of the first signs of maturity and women particularly don't mind asking for help. This one of the reasons women are three times more likely to succeed in business than men. When women know where they are going and get lost they wind down the window and ask for directions.

I emphasis this point because when I started my business I had the mistaken belief that asking for help could be seen as a sign of weakness when, in fact, it's a source of strength.

Since this time I've had invaluable help from all sorts of people but I prefer to ask people who are doing what I am about to attempt.

I call them people who have "walked the walk" Surrounding yourself with successful people like this will dramatically increase your chance of business success.

Each year I travel to Portland Oregon and spend three weeks with my Business Mentor David Gunderson. We are in regular contact by e-mail for the rest of the year too. My Sales mentor Russ Sheaf is now retired from selling in the pharmaceutical industry and is still a valuable source of advice.

Your Notes:

6 Why Start Your Own Small Business?

"No one knows how high you can fly until you spread your wings"

I started my own business to put bread on the table. Following five redundancies from the metal bashing industries in the 1980's I was fed up trying to find another job - so I started my own job. Many people who start in business this way don't own a business - they own a job! They are self-employed.

We believe 800,000 people in the UK fluctuate between self-employment and employment depending upon how well the economy is performing. This means between about 3.1 and 3.9 million Small Businesses exist at any one time.

When the economy is hot we get less Small Businesses and when the economy is cool we get more. This is because as more people get thrown out of work they seek the dream of owning their own business. However when the economy improves most of these entrepreneurs, fed up with working all hours for little reward, go back to a "proper job" working for someone else.

Some people start in business after a fight with the boss. At 55 years of age my friend Terry refused to unload a lorry in the rain. His boss was half his age and there had been tension between them for some time. Terry walked out. He hired a machine in the corner of a factory and went on to build a very profitable tool making firm employing over 30 highly skilled toolmakers.

Others start businesses because of family tradition. Like Kuldip whose father was a dentist in Bombay and then in Kenya. Kuldip was trained overseas as a dentist like his father before him and currently runs three dental practices in Kent. Kuldip was over 50 when he arrived in the UK.

Colonel Sanders started Kentucky Fried Chicken when he was 60 because he couldn't live on his pension. He was a billionaire by the time he was 80.

There are as many reasons for starting in business as there are people in business but perhaps the right reason for starting a business is that:

"You have an idea and a passion to serve someone better than they are now being served"

7 Women in Business

Women in Business

After helping over 25,000 start up businesses I've listed the 7 main reasons why women are more successful in business:

1. They know that business is about serving others.
2. They don't mind asking for help.
3. They know how to network
4. They are usually better at multi-tasking.
5. They know that humility works and arrogance doesn't
6. They tend to have a more Co-operative management style
7. They tend to have better budgeting skills and they also make their money work harder. For instance Joan, the first IT Consultant I worked with, decided to go for second and third hand furniture for her office. She knew the customer would never see it. She spent the savings on professionally designed stationary and marketing materials.

In the mean time Tim, a Quality Consultant, bought a top of the range car arguing he had to "appear successful."

There were other factors involved but today Joan is doing very nicely while Tim is having trouble making the payments on his car

8 Seven Benchmarks to Business Success

Over the years I have observed businesses that worked and businesses that didn't. Most of the ones that worked followed what I call the 7 benchmarks to business success.

1. Discovery of a viable market segment
They all found a group of people who were discontent. They then offered to solve the customers' problems with a novel product or service.

2. Formation of a well oiled team
Sometimes called a Mastermind Group. From the early days in business the founders worked together on problems and also had separate areas of specialty E.G Sales, Production, Finance, Research and Development etc. One person was assigned to be responsible for each area of the business.

3. Attraction of Investment Capital
Venture capitalists and banks look for mouthwatering professional presentations. They are also very interested in benchmarks 1. & 2. From my own observations I would rate a start up has 85% chance of success with just the first two benchmarks in place. They are also vitally important ingredients in attracting Investment Capital.

4. Market Penetration
Successful businesses build a sales machine or process to get better market penetration. Sales teams, well managed with financial incentives, are usually a key component in successful Start-ups. A good Sales

Manager knows top salespeople also have ego needs and these need to be catered for too.

5. Growth to Industry Leadership
By listening to the customer and finding what the customer wants but is not getting, new improved products and services were developed. By incrementally improving the customer's perception of their services businesses soon became market leaders.

6. Work/Life Balance of the Owner Managers
Many owner managers became workaholics. They were saying that they "loved" their work - which I took as a danger sign. Many were working over 55 hours a week. Some of these went on to divorce. Others literally worked themselves to death and others used alcohol and drugs to manage their stress. These people did not own a business - the business owned them! The really successful Owner Manager put balance before everything else.

7. Provision of an exit strategy
If goals drive us forward then an exit strategy pulls. It is rightly argued that when building a business we should build it so one day we will be able to sell it.

Obviously we should build the business so it works when we don't - because when we come to leave the business will sell better.

Your Notes:

Which Business?

"Do what you love to do and the money will follow"

A golden rule in business is to "Find out what your customers want (and are not getting) and supply it at a profit" It does not matter what industry or service you apply this rule - it always works. This book talks about providing products or services. As far as this book is concerned these terms are interchangeable. Don't get hung up on either and keep an open mind. Many businesses start out providing a service and end up also providing products and visa - versa.

"Whatever business you decide to do, to be successful you must start looking through your customers eyes"
Ask them what they want!

Service Industry or Manufacturer?

It is often easier and cheaper to start a business providing a service because mostly all you need is excellence and a few selling skills. This is the main reason for the phenomenal growth in service industries in the UK and one of the reasons for the demise of the manufacturing sector.

Many people have a bundle of skills acquired over the years. If you can find what other skills are needed (perhaps finance and sales) and you get them, you can start a manufacturing or service business.

Your Notes:

10 Lifestyle Businesses

Some people reading this book will not want to build a business but simply want several mini incomes to supplement their merge pensions or enough money to tide them over until they retire. You can also relieve yourself from a lot of worry supporting your wants and needs, while you are plowing your business Start-Up profits back into your business.

This book is about business so let us look at other ways of earning money rather than working for someone else. I call them Mini Incomes but other people often refer to them as Lifestyle Businesses.

Mini Incomes

My wife's Grandfather retired four times from various jobs and finally finished work well over 80 years of age. Like a lot of working people Ike never visualised himself "running a business" but "selling his labour" He was perfectly happy just doing a part time job.

Lifestyle Businesses are not a part time job!

There is no excuse for the average qualified Britain not to earn £20 an hour from his or her evenings or weekends. But the income must have seven criteria to qualify as a mini income.

1. Each mini income must be enjoyable and fit in with your lifestyle.
2. Each should produce a minimum of £20 an hour for every hour you invest.

3. Once the mini income is working well and efficiently let someone else run it to free yourself to build your business or find and develop other mini incomes.
4. Each mini income should be continuous so you can lean on the profits while you quit your full time job to begin your start up.
5. Each mini income should give you £500 per year in cash reserves.
6. You will be surprised how many opportunities will become apparent once your mindset is orientated to look for them! Use my "Wheel of Fortune" (Page 30) to start you off. Use some of the criteria above on the wheel.
7. Many readers will simply carry on developing more and more Mini Incomes and forget about the business start up. This is not the intention of this section but may offer useful ideas for some.

Examples:
Craft Fairs, e-bay, newspaper ads, - Anywhere people spend money…!

Your Examples:

11 S.W.O.T. Analyse Yourself

SWOT is a short way of saying Strengths, Weaknesses, Opportunities, and Threats. This is a useful marketing tool. Do one for yourself by substituting your information in the following:

SWOT ANALYSIS - QUALITY CONSULTANT

Strengths: 27 years industrial experience including 4 as production manager. Implemented ISO 9002 in two factories. 2 good contacts. Low overheads. Member British Institute of Managers.

Weaknesses: Not trained as an assessor. No reputation as a consultant. Dislikes selling. No office or telephone support. Little or no capital. Little sales experience.

Opportunities: Huge market potential. Big firm insisting suppliers become accredited. New firms may need ISO9002

Threats: Ageism, Sexism. Economic recession. Vast number of competitors. Feast & Famine because it is difficult to sell while working on a current project.

12 Wheel of Fortune

Here is a problem-solving tool that can solve most business problems. I call it my wheel of fortune:

Take an A4 sheet of paper.

1. Draw a 50mm circle in the center.
2. Put 10 short spokes from the hub of the problem.
3. State the problem in block capitals in the circle.
4. At the end of each spoke put a component of the problem.

Note! We are not thinking of an answer and listing its parts - we are doing the opposite I.e. Listing the parts in order to find the answer.

Remember: One of the better ways of starting a business is to find out what you're really passionate about and then find away to make a living at it!

Your notes:

Using the wheel of fortune to find my ideal business:

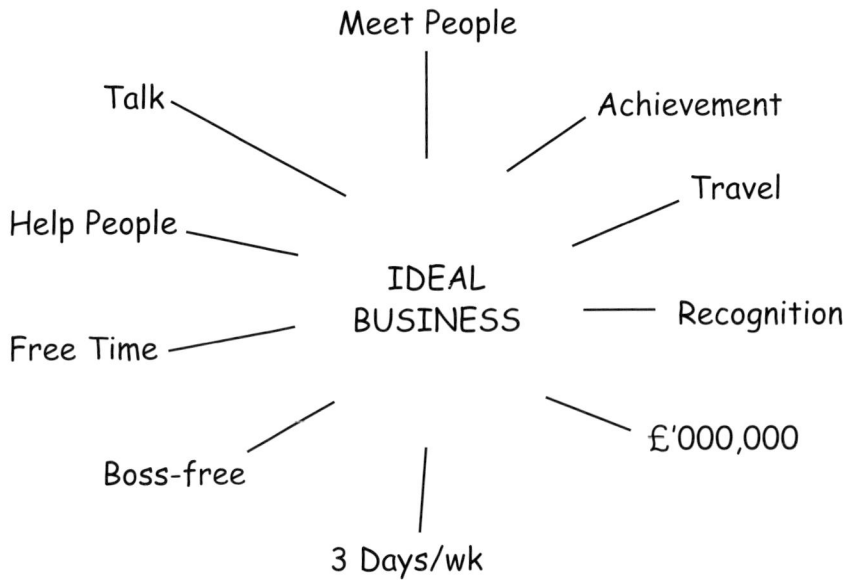

Put your wheel on the wall by your bed and hand over the problem to your subconscious by saying out loud: "OK brain give me the answer in three days time"...Have a paper and pen handy to capture the idea when it arrives because it will arrive!

There is nothing "mysterious" about how this works. Your brain is a very powerful computer that works in pictures and you've turned the problem into a picture. Just relax and your mindset will do the rest.

The Wheel works with most business problems such as "How do I reduce costs? Increase sales, Improve cash flow etc. So use it often.

Stick to what you know best?

With having to learn so many new business skills perhaps it's best to choose a business with which you are already familiar…

"Stick to the knitting" as they say in the textile industry.

Sir Richard Branson is one of our greatest entrepreneurs and he has many different businesses.

He is an exception. For every entrepreneur like him there are literally thousands who have failed because they have moved into areas they do not fully understand. Many businesses in financial trouble are "Now concentrating on core business" which is a phrase the directors use instead of, "How the hell did we get so far off track and lose so much money?"

Delight Your Customers

Can you find a product or service where you can delight your customers? Perhaps a niche serving specialist markets?

It is no longer good enough just to satisfy a customer. Anybody can satisfy a customer. If you only satisfy a customer you will soon watch your customer flying to a competitor who is prepared to delight them.

Today we have to delight customers. As no one can delight everybody, I suggest you stick to a group of people you know well enough to delight.

A young man I know was trained as a Doctor. Both of his parents were Doctors but he failed his finals so took the first job to come along. He sold insurance. After I had a chat with him about niche marketing he decided to specialise in selling insurance to Doctors. Today he is not only happier but is earning fifteen times more than his nearest rival.

Generalists always end up competing on price but specialists can start to earn some serious money...

E.g. Most car breakers make a good living but the ones who specialise on, say, Ford Focus, have lots of customers and charge a top price for their spares.

I've specialised in small business seminars and am a big fish in a small market. I even have a web site: www.Over50.Biz - you should visit it!

Whatever business you decide to do - commit to being the best!

What to call it?

"A rose by any other name is not the same"

I remember toying for hours with my business name and designing the letterheads. My time would certainly been better spent making contacts and getting sales. Make no mistake though the name you choose is the most important marketing decision you will make.

Can you name your business what you do? "Focus Parts and Panels" for example? Try not to name it after yourself - call it what you do. This is part of your tactics when positioning.

Positioning

"Positioning is what you do to your customers mind"

This is the most effective way to communicate in an over communicated society. On average your customer receives 250,000 advertising messages a year. Positioning is the art of being first in your customers' mind when he needs your product or service. Your business name is vital in the positioning war. Get the .com or. co.uk version of your name for the Internet too!

If you can be first in the market with a new idea and have an appropriate name (Like Red Bull for instance) everyone who follows after you, even with a better product or service, will always be lower on the ladder in your customers mind.

I've actually seen people standing at a Kodak photocopier asking staff how to make a Xerox copy on this machine...

Your Notes:

13 Market Research and Pricing

"How to find the hole and fill it"

In every market there are diamonds just waiting to be found. The diamonds are in your customer's head. It takes market research to dig them out.

"You have two ears and one mouth. Use them in that proportion when dealing with your customers..."

If you ask your customers the right questions in the right way and listen carefully to the answers you will come up with a piece of information that can literally transform your business. It's the rough diamond many people look for but rarely find. **You must learn to ask the right questions!**

Industry Gap Analysis

There are many worn out tired industries and one of the entrepreneurs marketing tricks is to enter the market where the demand is large and the competition is worst. Look for the segment of the market which are the most unhappy with the product or service.

Recently so-called budget airlines have made a killing in the UK by using Industry Gap Analysis. British Airways was the dominant player in the UK for years. Anywhere you have a large, bureaucratic, slow to turn industry, a quick to make decisions, low cost Start Up can be well established for years before the competition even know you are there.

Customer Gap Analysis

Most people will be familiar with this method. Businesses are always conducting market research surveys to spot a new gap. Listen closely to your customer. One enterprising hairdresser is offering sun beds, nail extensions and horoscopes!

Distribution Gap Analysis

You have a product or service but how best can you get it to market? Look for spaces in your customer's day where they are standing around with money in their pockets.

Supermarkets in the UK suddenly realised that petrol forecourts were an ideal place to sell more goods to more people. They bought in their retail expertise and the result is history.

My own experience

In my own case I was running business seminars for Small Businesses and I couldn't get anyone to sponsor them. Small Businesses haven't much money so the trick is to get someone else to pay.
After one grueling seminar I asked a couple of guests from a Business Link why they wouldn't sponsor me? "We haven't time to market the seminars Tom" was the reply.

Since this time I market my own seminars - often getting over 100 delighted delegates to each event - and lots of sponsorship.

Can you apply this idea to your business? Ask a direct question of your customer then <u>shut up</u> and wait for the answer?

Market Research and Pricing

Of course when doing your market research one of your questions should always be: "What is the one thing your existing supplier could do better?" If you ask 100 potential customers you will get enough different answers to enable you to design a product or service that is refreshingly different. Innovation is a key to business success.

Innovate, Innovate, Innovate

James Dyson listened to his customers and produced a world beating vacuum cleaner and is now using the same listening technique on other domestic appliances.

Market research need not cost a fortune. A friend of mine came from Uganda when he was sixty years old. He had hardly a penny to his name. He rented a shop and his family cleaned it thoroughly.

There were hardly any goods in his shop but he was always friendly and polite. When a customer asked him for some goods he hadn't got he smiled and apologised and said "If you want to be a regular customer I'll gladly stock some for you" and at the checkout he always asked "Did you find everything you were looking for in the store today?"

By listening to his customer he gradually built a stock of fast moving items. Soon he was able to take over the shop next door expanding his range. Mr. Singh now has a string of small supermarkets across the West Midlands and is one of the most successful men I know. He achieved this by listening to his customers.

When you have a product or service designed by your customers how much can you charge for it? Like James Dyson and Mr. Singh - you can charge a premium price!

Research the competition

<u>This is vitally important!</u> Go out and pretend to be a customer of seven businesses supplying similar goods or services that you are proposing to supply. If you can't find seven ask Why? Why? Why?

If you have no competition - what are you missing here?

Note your competitor's colour schemes, store layout, prices, their promotions, their position in relation to the customers and the products they supply.

By copying the competition and upgrading what they do you can start your business at the top of the pile. By starting at the top it saves all that climbing.

Your Notes:

Pricing

Pricing is one area where big mistakes are made. Many owner/managers cannot sell so they "give it away" with low prices, justifying their low price on lower overheads.

My own rule of thumb is to "Charge as much as the market will stand - while showing the customer value for money"

Try this tool to determine your prices:

Draw a grid showing competitors prices against products.

Find the average price

Decide your selling price

Aim in the upper quartile

	Product A	**Product B**	**Product C**	**Product D**
Competitor 1 Prices £				
Competitor 2 Prices £				
Competitor 3 Prices £				
Totals	£	£	£	£
Totals ÷ 3 = Average Price	£	£	£	£
Now Decide Your Price	£	£	£	£

Experiment with your prices. If you cannot sell enough at one price put up the price to see if you can sell more at a higher price. Try using the numbers 7, 8 or 9 in your price as most people report a significant increase in sales.

E.g. My first business venture was selling battery chargers through an ad in the Daily Mail and I hardly sold any at discount prices. When I doubled the price I sold twice as many.

E.g. One consultant I know doubled his prices and lost half of his customers. He is a very happy man because he now earns the same money but for half the hours…

E.g. Supermarkets charge high for most items but customer "perception" is Supermarket prices are low.

Supermarket customers only know the price of about 20 products so if supermarkets keep those 20 prices low this gives the customer the perception that all of their prices are low. The Supermarket then charges higher prices for the other 30,000 or so items on the shelf.

People make buying decisions emotionally then they justify it with logic. If you can delight your customer by providing innovative quality products, to a niche market, quickly and cleanly you should charge a high price.

If you want to increase your prices - put them up in writing! This is because people believe the written word more than the spoken one. Just put up a new price list or print new tickets.

My friend told me that when he arrived in England he knew it was a land of golden opportunities because shopkeepers expected him to pay the price on the ticket. "Where I came from Tom, that price was only the starting point for the negotiations - at the retail level hardly anyone in England negotiates"

In life you don't get what you deserve - you get what you negotiate. So, finally, get on a negotiating course. You will negotiate more profit than you will ever earn.

Your notes on pricing:

14 The Different Types of Businesses

Sole Traders

This is the simplest way to start-up a business. No registration is required and no legal requirements to produce accounts only simple procedures are necessary. Once you are established you must pay tax sometime after your profits have been earned. Two words of warning here:

1. The Tax Man has closed more businesses and bankrupted more people than all others put together. Don't mess with these guys.
2. Keep all of your receipts and invoices and keep them in order. When an accountant looks at your books he will charge you by the hour and if it takes him 20 hours to sort out your receipts - expect a very large bill.

Sole traders have control over their own accounts and do not have to disclose information to the public but they do to the Inland Revenue.

Disadvantages of sole trader

There are disadvantages with running as a sole trader. You have little or no credibility when you first start and this is bad for sales and pricing but your ability to raise money is also affected.

The biggest disadvantage is that you, the owner, takes all the losses. You have unlimited liability. That is to say your home and everything you own is liable to be lost if things go seriously wrong.

How to set up as a sole trader in the UK

1. Go to the Business Link/Enterprise Support Agency.

2. Inform the local tax inspector and a new reference number will be given

3. And inform the local Contributions Agency (NI) at the same time.

4. Check with planning officer that premises are suitable. Can you work from home? Tip: Don't tell people you are running a business from home - tell them you are "working from home"

5. Check mortgage insurance etc

6. Open a separate bank account

7. If trading under a business name: letter headed paper required to show the bank, must show personal name and address.

8. Check the VAT implications.

Remember that asking for help is the first sign of maturity. This is particularly true when starting a business. Many failures are due to a "Know it all" attitude. I've been teaching this stuff for 30 years and I still don't know it all.

Keep it legal.

Personally I believe if you have to do anything dishonest or illegal to make money in a business you are not running it right. As someone recently asked: "Tom, what's the difference between tax avoidance and tax evasion? I answered "About 5 years!"

Your notes:

Partnerships

Catherine Zeta Jones married Michael Douglas and he insisted on a prenuptial agreement; if they divorced she wasn't entitled to half of everything he owned.

A marriage is a partnership and 40% of marriages fail. It certainly pays to think through the consequences if your partnership fails. I strongly recommend a legal business partnership agreement before trading starts. Even in a business partnership between a husband and wife! A Personal Business Advisor at Business Link or the Enterprise Agency could help you write up the agreement.

My advice is not to have a partnership but to set the business up as a Limited Company and allocate shares to the partners.

A partnership has advantages and disadvantages;

Advantages of partnerships

The main advantages of a sole trader also apply to a partnership I.e. No legal requirements to produce accounts, tax payable sometime after profits earned, etc. But partnerships have another advantage:

Pooling of effort and pooling of skills. Pick a partner who has the skills you don't have; as well as some of the skills you do.

Your notes:

Disadvantages of partnerships

The main disadvantages of a sole trader also apply to partnerships i.e. credibility and options to raise money limited etc. Plus two big disadvantages that sole traders don't have:

1. Your unlimited liability also apples to your partners debts and loses
2. The possibility of personality clashes!

How to set up as a Partnership

As a sole trader plus a partnership agreement is strongly recommended. In the event of a dispute the agreement covers date of partnership, capital, rate of interest, profit split, holidays, time off, retirement, death, dissolution of the partnership.

In the event of a dispute

Get around a table and resolve it yourselves, or go to arbitration. Do everything possible to avoid Lawyers and Courts to settle your disputes.

Limited Company

A Limited Company (Ltd.) is a separate legal person we create to give us advantages and protection. Most of the advantages revolve around credibility and tax and the protection revolves around not losing your shirt in the event of things going badly wrong.

However most banks or financial institutions will insist you sign a personal guarantee when you borrow money for the business. Signing a personal guarantee loses the protection that the Limited Company bought you.

Remember that when you set up a Limited Company you are now an employee and if you take money out you are stealing! I must emphasize this point because many people set up a company and use it like their own private piggy bank. Later they find themselves in trouble because they took what they thought was their own money.

It is not your money - it's the Company's money!

The advantages of a Limited Company are:

1. Limited liability so debts are usually limited to the amount paid for shares.

2. Options for raising finance can be greater

3. Tax advantages - see a good accountant.

The disadvantages of a limited Company are:

1. Audited accounts have to be produced and filed at Companies house.

2. Two lots of National Insurance have to be paid, one for the employer and one for the employee.

3. Tax has to be paid under the PAYE system and /or Corporation Tax.

How to set up as a limited company

1. Go to the Business Link / Enterprise Support Agency and ask for help

2. Get an Accountant and ask advice

3. Contact a solicitor or obtain a starter pack from Companies House

4. Get a Personal Business Advisor

5. Take documents to bank I.e. Memorandum of Association, Articles

of Association, Certificate of Incorporation etc.

6. Accountants and Lawyers for Enterprise schemes provide initial free advice, as does the Small Business Service.

7. Remember to chose an appropriate name from the file or get an existing company and change it's name.

Your notes:

15 Insurance and Pensions

A school friend of mine has been a market trader for over 25 years and was recently wiped out overnight by a fire. Keith thought the warehouse where he stored his stock had fire insurance to protect his stock and it didn't...

Insurance is an aspect of start up very often left until the business is established and then forgotten. Sufficient insurance is vital as soon as you have stock premises and so on before you start to trade. With the popular practice of suing anybody for anything even a self employed Consultant should get "Professional Indemnity Insurance"

Consider the following risks: **Employers Liability** - a legal requirement if you are employing people - Public Liability - To protect you from claims from members of the public from injuries received real or imagined!

Product Indemnity - Faulty instructions or faulty products can cause people to suffer and they can sue you. Professional Indemnity already mentioned. Doctors Lawyers Accountants Trainers etc are currently being sued for millions in damages.

Personal accident - many business people are too busy to have time off through illness but there are some illnesses and certainly accidents that can put you off work for months. Are you covered?

Key Person Income Protection - My cousin's partner died suddenly and it had a catastrophic effect on the business. KPIP insurance buys time while the problems are being sorted out.

Work From Home Policy - Your normal domestic insurance will not cover you working from home. This type of insurance is similar to an all risks policy.

Pensions

God willing we will all get really old one day so we should make financial provision for this. Contributions to pension plans and Retirement Annuities are tax deductible but of course we must make enough money in the first place to pay the contributions! It's better to get a flexible plan where you can increase or decrease in good years and bad. Personally I have invested in property because I never trusted pension companies to deliver.

Advice should be taken from a Financial Adviser or Insurance Broker. Your accountant too can show you ways of owning your own business property to tax advantage, which is a popular way of financing a pension.

The ultimate aim must be to become an investor. Investing in your own business can be one of the most profitable ways to invest your money but, like other forms of investment it also carries risk.

> **"Ordinary people work hard for money while rich people make their money work hard for them!"**

If you save as you earn at least 15% of your income, one day you will have a pot of money, the interest from which is big enough to support your weekly needs. The multiplier effect of compound interests helps here! Or, of course, invest in your own business!

16 All About Franchises

I always suggest to my older clients they visit a franchise exhibition. Not necessarily to buy a franchise but to look how the franchises operate. You'll always find a franchise offering similar products and services to you. Some people start their businesses by simply modeling and upgrading what the franchisers do.

Franchise is a great way of starting your business if you are over 50 because someone else has taken the time to develop a business model that works.

Bullet Proof Small Businesses

A franchise is a bulletproof small business. Over 90% of franchises are still operating 2 years after start up, compared to only 20% of people who started on their own.

The Franchiser has taken the trouble to research and experiment and document to build a prototype. A business that works. They then duplicate the model all over the UK and all over the world.

These are sometimes called "turn key" businesses - turn the door key, and the business works.

Fewer failures

Because of the support in terms of training, operations procedures, store formats, and advertising, franchises offer the greatest chance of success - But make no mistake - they still require hard work and a competitive spirit to make them work!

To make serious money through a franchise you will need multiple franchises but you can earn a very good living with just one.

Which Franchise?

Most franchises are bought on an emotional level because you like the food or service, which is important, but before signing on the dotted line, a lot of hard objective research should be undertaken to see if this franchise really is the right one for you. The British Franchise Association has a list of members - so start there.

1. Ask yourself "Can I visualise myself working 10 hours a day and still be happy doing this - every day?" Remember your customers can only be as happy as you and your staff!

2. Ride with at least one franchisee to see him servicing his customers, making cold calls, or attending meetings, to get a feel for the business.

3. Talk to his customers to see if there have been any problems with quality, service or delivery.

4. Talk with 5/6 franchisees and ask each one:

Ask the franchisee:

Do you still enjoy what you are doing? What don't you like about your franchise? Given your time again would you go into this business? What would you differently next time? Should it come available would you buy a second location? What's the support from the franchiser like? What are the product supply problems? Was the training useful to the start up? Is the franchiser responsive to problems and helps you sort them out? Have you had any encroachment problems with the franchiser selling a franchise that crosses your area? What are your gross sales per year?

What are the production costs? Is the business seasonal and if so how do you pay for the staff in the off season? Is the advertising any good? Are the promotional materials any good?

The next stop is the Business Link or Enterprise Agency asking for a Personal Business Advisor who has had experience with franchises. Also talk to a Franchise Officer at your Bank.

Construct a detailed Business Plan. Calculate a worst case scenario showing how low the sales can get before you cannot cover your weekly payments. (Break-even figure).

The Personal Business Advisor (PBA) will look at the small print in the contract. They will point out the Importance of location, the advisability of running a credit check on the franchiser, finding if the franchiser is a member of the British Franchise Association or not, how to negotiate a better price for the franchise, the stocks, the fees, the buildings, the decorations etc. (Remember: Everything is negotiable)

Recently I went to the British Franchise Exhibition and most Franchisees seem to pay between £4,000 - £40,000 for the deal but I know of one costing £750,000 about to be imported into Europe from the USA.

Final words of advice:

As a business speaker I've helped at many franchise conferences. I am always amazed at how quickly the new franchisee thinks he knows the business better than the company who has been in the business for years.

If you have paid a small fortune for a business that works why try to change it and do it your way? Stick to the system and work hard.

Don't expect to make money from day one. Pay your suppliers and staff first. And, as with any business, your biggest asset is location, location, location!

Your notes:

17 How to Build Better Business

Maybe you just want to be a sole trader or run a lifestyle business but I strongly suggest you still design and build your business the same way as if you were going to grow it. Your business is like a child. Once you have given birth believe me it will grow despite what you want. It's a simple business truth that you cannot stay the same size. However resist the pressure to grow too fast. <u>Get better before you get bigger.</u>

A money harvesting machine

My definition of a successful business is: "A money harvesting machine" This section is about building such a machine for yourself.

How to build a money harvesting machine

Essentially it will consist of three machines, the fourth can be added later.

1. A production or service machine.

2. A sales & marketing machine.

3. The finance machine, controlling money coming in and going out.

4. A business-duplicating machine (expansion system)

All businesses with more than one successful outlet have built a system dedicated to expansion.

"The system is the solution" - AT&T

Graphically your small business will look like this:

Your Small Business
As a Money Harvesting Machine

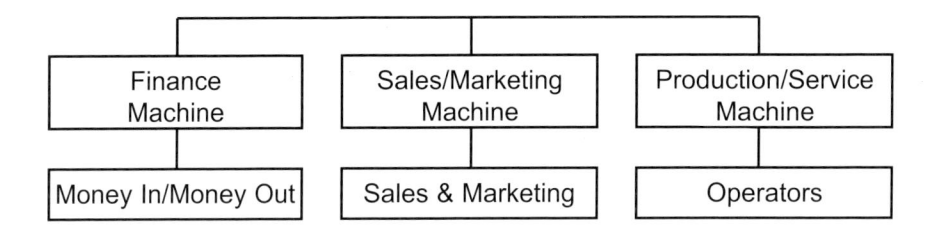

```
     ┌──────────────┬──────────────────┬──────────────────┐
     │              │                  │                  │
┌──────────┐  ┌──────────────┐  ┌──────────────────┐
│ Finance  │  │Sales/Marketing│  │Production/Service│
│ Machine  │  │   Machine     │  │    Machine       │
└──────────┘  └──────────────┘  └──────────────────┘
     │              │                  │
┌──────────────┐ ┌──────────────┐ ┌──────────────┐
│Money In/Money Out│ │Sales & Marketing│ │  Operators  │
└──────────────┘ └──────────────┘ └──────────────┘
```

Production/Service Machine

My car mechanic bought his business after retiring from the RAF. In the RAF he maintained fighter planes now he maintains cars.

He didn't buy a business - he bought a job! In fact he is the job and I can tell he is getting disillusioned with working all hours and he's not getting any younger...

My local stationer started his second shop in Wolverhampton after starting his first in another town. It wasn't too long before he closed one because he couldn't be in two places at one time.

What both examples have in common is that the owner should have worked <u>on</u> the business as well as <u>in</u> the business.

Both mechanic and stationer are too busy "doing work" to build a business. Often owner managers are too busy working to make any money!

Both small businesses need:

An Organisation Chart to show what the business will look like when they've finished building it in, let's say, 3 years. How many employees - doing what and so on…

Operating Manuals for each position on a chart so the owner/manager can duplicate themselves and get consistent product or service from new staff.

Operating checklists or manuals will be training manuals for the new employees to duplicate what the owner/manager found works with his customers.

Budgets Simple, adequate, control information with realistic targets to help run the business. Perhaps In the form of a picture for ease of understanding.

Start at the bottom of the chart and pick an operators job. Analyse and experiment until you find out what works with your customers then lock it into the manual. The manual can be a simple tick box sheet or more complex. Perhaps colour coded for each department.

My own operating manual, for my one-man business, tells the philosophy behind the business and is a series of checklists for each seminar. Included are instructions for listening to a tape on the topic on the way to the event, room layout, speaking to members of the audience before the event and what to say.

The drawing of a mind map immediately before the event, the script, key points, conclusion, thanking the sponsors etc. Are all included. Anyone with my manual can perform as well, if not better than me.

What you do is a performance too..

It's a performance that can be scripted and stage set so whoever runs it can get the same results as you. It's only ego if you think no one else can do it better than you.

When you have reduced what you do to a performance then your staffs' personality will bring the performance to life. Hire staff that naturally smile at customers as you can train them to do nearly everything else..

You can see how my seminars are a theatrical performance. Can you see what you do is also a performance? In this ever-changing world customers crave consistency - give it to them.

Next to profits the most important goal a business should strive for is consistency.

The same sort of consistency that a machine produces parts. Parts that are similar to within a thousandth of a centimeter.

At business start up I strongly recommend all businesses have an organisation chart, operating manuals or checklists and budgets.

Your notes:

18 The Sales/Marketing Machine

Sales

Even if you have enough sales now the market <u>will</u> move. The market always moves.

Recently I analysed my income and found 58.5% of my income came from two linked groups of customers. This is dangerous so I wheeled out my sales machine and applied it to new markets. I was just ahead of the game because both groups of old customers went into a tailspin about the same time.

Imagine what would have happened if I hadn't kept my sales machine ready, oiled and fueled? Or worse still, not had a sales machine at all?

To build your own sales machine first decide how much money you want to make during the forthcoming year and convert this income figure into numbers and value of sales.

To hit my financial target next year I need to find two new customers every month while keeping 97% of my existing business.

To get two new customers a month I write 4 proposals. (Solutions to customers problems) I need 8 fact-finding visits (FFV) to write 4 proposals. 20 direct mail letters followed up with a phone call gets me the 8 visits I need to get eyeball to eyeball with my prospects.

So every month, <u>without fail</u>, I send 20 letters and make 20 phone calls, visit 8 prospects and write 4 proposals.

On average this takes 4 days every month (and would cost a total of £2400 if I included the cost of my time.)

Graphically it looks like this:

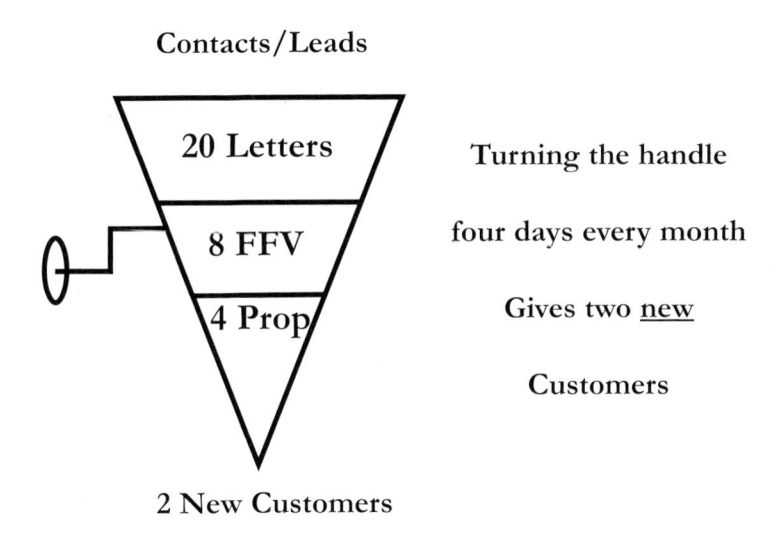

Contacts/Leads

20 Letters — Turning the handle

8 FFV — four days every month

4 Prop — Gives two <u>new</u> Customers

2 New Customers

In the USA Dave Gunderson, my business mentor, manages a national sales team and uses nine criterions with which to measure the effectiveness of each salesman. They all report to him daily on the intranet. By the evening he knows who is "on system" and who is not.

In each criterion he puts the bottom performer with the top performer for training, so building the synergy of the whole team. He calls this criterion Key Performance Indicators, (KPIs) others call them benchmarks.

Over the years I've experimented at each level of my own sales machine to find what works and what doesn't and I've written it down in my sales manual.

For instance I've found I get 11.5% better response from my letters if I have the heading in inverted commas and also write a hand written PS. in dark blue ink.

I get a massive 46% better response at the fact finding visit stage when I wear a blue suit and ask the "industry special" questions I've developed over the years.

I can hear you saying, "I don't get my new customers this way - so this doesn't apply to me!"

WRONG!

Adapt and apply

Adapt and make this apply to your business. For instance:

How about placing your adverts in a different section of the newspaper? Or Yellow pages? With a picture? Without? Higher price?

Do you get a better response to your leafleting when you send 333 houses the same leaflet 3 times - or 1000 houses one leaflet?

Do you have a counting device to tell you how many people come into your shop? Have you measured the difference in sales when you ask, "How can I help you?" compared with "Can I help you?" What impact does eye contact and a smile make?

Advertising only gets you shoppers. It is your sales skills that will turn them into customers!

It is important to go on a personal selling skills course and if it includes negotiating you are two up.

Coming from a production background I almost despised sales people. So how can you become something you despise? The answer is to love your product or service.

My definition of a sale is "*The transfer of enthusiasm from you to the prospect*" The more enthusiasm the more sales and also the greater the ability to ignore the no's!

It was only when my business was going down the pan that I asked for help. Russ is a top salesman with a chemists supply company. I asked him for help and he helped me enormously. He taught me that sales are a numbers game and direct sales are the result of confidence using questioning techniques. This is the subject of my other book *but you will question your way into far more sales than you could ever talk your way into.*

Sales is the only profession I know where questions are the answer... Questions like: What? Why? Where? How? When? Who? Used with skill can generate dozens of sales.

Find out what people want and supply it at a profit.

Find out by asking questions - then help customers buy.

See five brand new contacts everyday and enthusiastically tell them your story and you will see sales boom.

Your notes:

19 Marketing Plan

Marketing has been dealt with in depth in my book "*How to market advertise and promote your small business or service*" but I want briefly show you the main points again - also remember: Location Location and Location i.e. Where are your customers?

The Marketing Plan Contents:

Write a marketing plan. Included should be:

1. Business CV
2. SWOT analysis
3. Sales forecasting
4. Who and where are your customers?
5. Design a marketing calendar
6. How will you Advertise & promote?

Key Marketing Words

Do you have a **THEME** running through your business, colour coordinated and uniform? Give your customers a **DELIGHTFUL** shopping **EXPERIENCE**.

Have a Unique Selling Point **(USP)** that your competitors cannot copy. Form a **CUSTOMER PARTNERSHIP** helping them to achieve their goals. **MODEL** and existing highly successful business and

UPGRADE what they do. Give your customers **GOOD FEELINGS** and they'll keep coming back. **POSITION** yourself in your customers mind to be the first supplier they call.

MEGA-MARKETING

This is asking your customer what they will need in 6 -12 months time and, to stay ahead of the competition, you start developing this new product or service now!

In my own case I saw the advent of the Small Business Service so while on holiday in the USA and researched their best practice. The Small Business Administration has been running for years and is a highly successful system.

I've adapted many SBA ideas to my training and now run the best Business Seminars in the UK. Look at my web site www.tomedge.co.uk for lots of FREE help and 101 free hot tips.

Soon the competitors will copy but I'm already working on mark II seminars and workshops.

Spotting the trends

At the time of writing most customers are splitting into two main camps.

One group is going for trade names and aspiration brands and the other is looking for discounts. Middle market players are being squeezed out. So much so there may be room soon for middle market players…

Quick thinking retailers who champion the customer will certainly win more business. Larger firms are using "Trend Spotters" to see what's cool in the marketplace so they can stock them too.

Seasonal shops selling Christmas trees, Christmas lights, fireworks etc. Open for only 10 weeks can make up to 80% of the total yearly profits of typical News Agent! They don't have to get up at dawn and open seven days a week either.

Remember it is not enough just to put your goods in some shop window (advertise) and wait for someone to buy them. We must be proactive in selling. Businesses will get a lot more browsers in future and your sales skills and patience will need to be honed to turn browsers into customers. This is one of the problems with web based businesses, too many browsers not enough buyers.

Your notes:

20 Your Finance Machine

Most owner managers hate doing the books so they give them someone else to do. Anybody else! This is a fundamental mistake because if you are the chief spender and chief income generator you need to know daily if you are meeting your break even or not.

Many people have trouble reading a cash flow forecast because untrained brains work in pictures not numbers.

I suggest you have pie charts showing money coming in and money going out. Get your Accountant or Personal Business Adviser to help you set this up with easy to use software.

Simple, adequate control information will help you keep out of financial difficulties and are certainly worth the effort of setting up the systems at the start of your business.

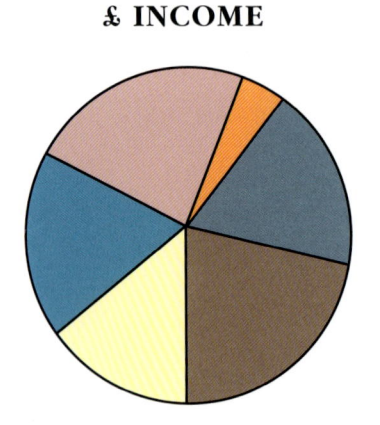

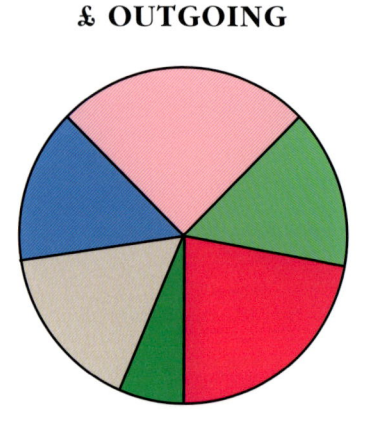

£ INCOME £ OUTGOING

...And those large wedges of pie show:

1. When too much of your income comes from too few customers.
2. Your biggest costs so you can reduce them.

Also set up a simple system of budgets showing weekly targets and if you are exceeding them. A one sheet budget is enough for most small businesses.

We cannot be expert at everything so we employ specialists or get partners who have strengths we do not. Make sure they are communicating information to you simply so you can use it to control your business.

People use graphs for sales and for finance. You can spot trends so much easier with a graph than a spread sheet and if you have a colour printer even better:

The sales graph is a lot easier to understand than data and it contains the same information...

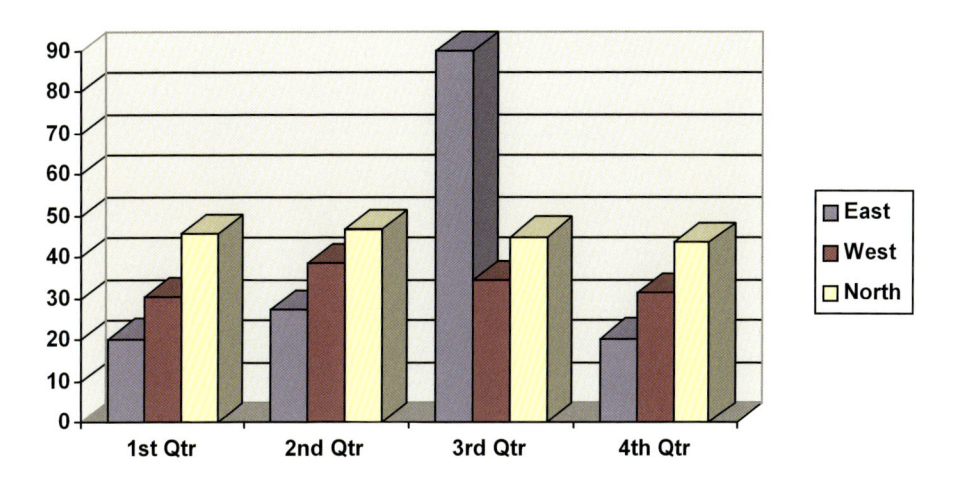

	1st Qtr	2nd Qtr	3rd Qtr	4th Qtr
East	20.4	27.4	90	20.4
West	30.6	38.6	34.6	31.6
North	45.9	46.9	45	43.9

Now you have the outlines of your three machines. When they run harmoniously together they form a "Money harvesting machine"

Your notes:

21 Internet Businesses

Some people really believe you can get something for nothing. This has fueled the success of The National Lottery and the phenomenal growth in suing people for accidents. It has also fueled the growth in DOTCOMS or as I prefer to call some of them DOTCONS and many will soon be DOTGONES owing thousands of investors millions of pounds.

I don't believe in Father Christmas or the Tooth Fairy and I've never believed the hype about the web because it mostly goes against sound business practice.

In an article written for a business magazine (See it at www.tomedge.co.uk New Rules for the New Retail Economy) I conclude that Internet shopping is likely to be popular for the purchase of digital and commodity products and tickets but not for fashion or those where the experience of the purchase is important.

(B2B) Business to Business trading is likely to be significant and People to People Sales (E-Bay) but (B2C) Business to Consumer or e-tail, not for quite a while. If we can add people to the technology we will have a winning formula.

Where we can now score with the web is to use it as another shop window in addition to our existing promotions and outlets. Names already known and trusted in the high street where the ones who scored first of course.

People, generally, will see the ad, research it on the net or in a catalogue, go and pick it up in the car - or perhaps get it delivered.

Large firms will rely on technology but customers want touch. This provides your Small Business with a window of opportunity. People like to buy from people and hate instructions from a tape recorder or a machine. If you can take the edge off the technology and replace it with human "touch" I believe you are on a winner. This is why E-Bay works so well - it is people to people selling.

If enough people have good experiences shopping on line it will suddenly take off like fax machines and mobile phones. In that case here are a few suggestions about Internet Businesses but remember the successful ones have spent years and lots of money fine-tuning their web presence.

<u>Get a great Website</u> and make sure you market it. Personalise it, make it friendly. Get a clear understanding of what you want the site to do. Sell? Promote your business? Pass on information? Attract new customers? Offer add-ons?

Set a realistic budget and an on going budget for refresher costs.

Surf and visit other sites. Use the latest ideas but if they're from the US you may have to adjust them before use. Visit your competitor sites and "borrow" their ideas. Don't forget to ask your customers for feedback too.

Design your Website as an order taker, marketing company, public relations consultant and information resource for your business. Show pictures of people happily using your products and show testimonials. Customers trust customers so your site should show your customers recommending your business.

The biggest reason for Internet business failure is because of slow loading home pages so forget the bells and whistles if they take to long to load. The second and third biggest reasons for failure are again to do with time. The time it takes to respond to the inquiry and the time it take to deliver the goods. You have to be quick in this business! 80% of purchases are abandoned while customers still are filling the shopping trolley!

Have a look at my site. There are several ways in but www.Over50.Biz will get you there.

Your notes:

22 The Business Plan

"If you don't know where you're going you are never going to get there"

Once you have visualised what your business will look like in 3 years and decided your personal goals, the business plan is your map to get you there. If you refer to it daily you will soon see when you are getting lost. And when you are lost? Simply wind the window down and ask directions. Personal Business Advisors, Mentors, Bank Managers, Accountants, Salespersons, etc. all will help if you ask.

Listen to the ones who have walked the walk. Many can talk the talk but only a few have walked the walk. Many know the theory but only a few the practices. Ask "Can you do me a favour and tell me how to ……..?"

Ask several people the same question and get a consensus before you make the decision. Keep it simple and don't go in for complicated ideas.

Trust your instincts. You haven't survived this long without developing a keen sixth sense so listen to that little voice within - what's it saying?

If something looks too good to be true it usually is. Yet only recently I got sucked into a telephone scam that cost me a few pounds. It knocked my confidence for weeks though to think I could get robbed that way. Yes there are crooks out there but don't let that blind you to all the good guys and girls who are honestly trying to help their customers. As one old businessman told me once in Istanbul,

"Trust in God but tie up your camels"

The best way of tying things up is to put them in writing. Write a business plan.

Your notes:

Shaping your Business Plan

"Keep it simple" A business plan is simply a series of about 10 sections that explain your idea and how you plan to make it work. Included should be:

1. Introduction
2. Your Skills and Experience
3. The Market
4. The Product/Service
5. Premises
6. Marketing Plan
7. Operations
8. Time Management
9. Financial Aspects
10. Contingency Plans

Initially this looks like a lot of writing but a single paragraph will cover most sections - and a page or two most others.

You will also need a Cash Flow Forecast as an Appendix and maybe some photographs or sketches to aid understanding. Get help with these from a Business Adviser.

I strongly recommend you include an organisation chart to show how the business will look in 3 years when you have finished building it.

Have the Business Plan typed to look good when you are presenting it to get finance or grants. Save it on disc to make any changes easier and lay it out professionally.

To create anything:

We have an **IDEA** or some creative impulse.

VISUALISE in our minds eye how it will look finished.

With the end in mind, **PLAN** on paper how to do it.

BUILD A MODEL or prototype to see if it works.

DO IT for real.

The formula is to build your castles in the air and then build the foundations up to them!

Your Notes:

Business Plan Contents Page

1. Introduction
2. Skills and Experience
3. The Market
4. The Product/Service
5. Premises
6. Marketing Plan
7. Operations
8. Time Management
9. Financial Aspects
10. Contingency Plans

1. Introduction

Who are you?

What is your business?

When was it first envisaged?

What are your aims and objectives?

What market research have you done?

What are your conclusions?

How will you fund it?

2. Skills and Experience

Track record.

Past achievements

Qualifications

Your motivation

Long term   - Staff/Family - What skills - Time scale?

3. The Market

Geographical

Sociological

Technical

Economic

Population trends

Size

Segment   -Who is your customer?
                      -What do they buy?

Competitors   -Who? Size? Reputation?
                      -Where are they?
                      -Price Compare?
                      -What's their likely response
                      ...and can you cope?

4. The Product or Service

Be specific and give detail - highlight any unique features

Photographs - portfolio - prototype

Use simple terms - If technical then compile an appendix

What do others think?

How will it develop?

What are your expectations of price?

How well will it stand in the market on price and appeal?

Breach of patent or copyright?

5. Premises

Image? Home? Rent? Lease? Buy? Position, Position, Position!

How close are your customers?

How many pass the door? (Count them!)

Parking? Transport?

How close are Competitors? Suppliers?

6. Marketing Plan

Getting Started

Now that we've established a Small Business perspective, create some marketing strategies for your business.

A marketing plan is a part of your overall business plan. I usually recommend that 30/40% of your business plan should be devoted to how you are going to market your business. Your marketing plan is one major area that Bank Managers and Venture Capitalists take a real close look at before lending you any money. They are very curious how you will attract customers, make sales, make a profit and pay them back on their investment in your business. We will use some of the information from the Business Plan in our Marketing Plan, but the Marketing Plan is usually its own entity within the Business Plan. If you don't have a Business Plan started yet, do that first. The Business Link or Enterprise Agency can offer free help to get you started. Find them in the phone book. Also check out your local Chamber of Commerce.

Marketing Plan

Cover in great depth 30-40% of the whole business plan

Get help or at least buy my book on this topic.(See order form P89)

How will you trade? (Sole Trader, Partnership, Ltd. Co?)

Trading name? - Hint: Call it what you do!

Selling price? - Hint: Try to charge in the upper quartile!

How did you determine your price?

Image, LOGO, Positioning?

How will you observe market changes?

State trading terms on invoices! Cash? 30/60 days credit? Cash flow?

Premises

Distribution

The longer term

New products

Advertising: What? Who is the target? Where? When? How?

7. Operations (Production?)

How is the business to be structured? (Organisation chart)

How is the product made or the service provided?

Quality control?

Manpower requirements and availability (who/what matrix)

Any missing skills?

How do you overcome these?

8. Time Management - Is vitally important!

I have never known a successful entrepreneur who did not operate from some personal organisation system.

Every morning: List jobs & then rewrite them in priority.

Use a year planner on the wall to get an overview

Book time off and holidays first then work around these.

Balance your work/home life using the planner!

Having a daily list saves me from two pests - hurry and indecision. It also keeps me on track towards my big dream. I've turned my goals into a picture for my wall, so I'm reminded of my goals every morning. I call this my "treasure map…"

Material things are relatively easy to get using a treasure map.

9. Financial aspects

What is your break-even figure?

How much money is required?

Likely source of funding?

Grants/loans? Ask the Small Business Service!

Equipment - Lease? Hire? Buy?

Cost of supplies - Ongoing review for better deals

Produce a cash flow forecast see Small Business Service

Listen to the advice from the bank & negotiate bank rates

Don't use loan sharks

Don't borrow money to get out of debt

10. Contingency plans

Conduct a "What if…?" Analysis

Sales below forecast? Key person is ill? Orders too large? Etc.

End of Business Plan

Your Notes:

23 Special Considerations For The Over 50s

We who are over 50 must take some extra precautions against stress, burnout, and Illnesses. We must also use tools to balancing our work with the rest of our lives.

In my own case I had a medical check up and was amazed how high my cholesterol and blood pressure were. A few pills, a healthier diet and exercise soon bought these down. I now exercise every morning for 20 minutes before work and business. Today I feel really great!

It is important to start your business feeling refreshed and healthy. So these days I do not go to bed at 'stupid o'clock'. Aim to get a minimum of 7.5 hours sleep and 30 minutes 'quiet time' in the afternoon. We know this already but frequently 'lie' to ourselves how fit we are for work.

Listen to your partner and listen to your instincts on this, as they are both usually right!

It is also important to have other outside interests as well as your business. Often a new venture can become all-consuming and as a potential workaholic myself, I can assure you all accesses must be paid for - sometimes at frightful cost. (I've lost too many friends to stress related heart attacks, divorce etc.) With this in mind you should try to separate home from work. This is difficult when you are working from home but essential for a balanced life. At home we do not talk about work after 6.00 p.m. and I physically lock the office door at that time too!

It also pays to have a phone line for home and a separate one for business. Put your answer machine on and the ring volume down at 6.00 p.m. Working only three days a week helps me enjoy my life and having regular weekends away works well too. Book your holidays just as soon as you put up your year planer and learn to negotiate time for your loved ones.

Learn to say "NO!" Especially to low profit, high maintenance customers and, perhaps the most important of all, know when to quit!

Your Notes:

My Health goals: **My Family Goals:**   **My Earning Goals:**

24 Where To Go For Help

Accountancy ICAEW: 01908-248090

British Franchise Association: 01491-578049

BNI Networking Organisation: Local directory

Business Link/Enterprise Agency: 0845 600 9006

Chambers of Commerce:

Internet:

Library Business Reference section:

PRIME (Over 50s Enterprise): 020 8765 7833

PRIME Website: www.primeinitiative.org.uk

My website: www.tomedge.co.uk (Hot Tips Section)

Business Insight: www.bestforbusiness.com

Business Eye: www.businesseye.co.uk

25 101 Final Thoughts

Don't name a business after yourself call it what you do.

A good business is a three-legged stool with production sales and finance legs in perfect balance.

Change your letterheads every three years or you'll be out of date.

I get 18.5% more sales when I wear a blue suit instead of a brown one and 1.5% more when I have red in my tie.

Don't look too flashy. Drive the same car as your customers - leave the Jaguar at home.

Spend 10 minutes every morning in Silence Stillness and Solitude to focus your creativity.

Power of 10 brain storming use the Wheel of Fortune to solve any business problem. (Pages 30-31)

Specialise and charge top price (but justify it as "value for money")

Upgrade your business by seeing who is making the most money and copy it. (People think you have to start at the bottom - you don't)

Ignore recessions. Just triple your sales effort. If you think there is a recession you put less effort into selling and it becomes a self-fulfilling prophecy.

Pin up a "treasure map" on your office wall. I.e. cut out pictures of your goals and dreams from magazines.

Put them where you can see them daily. Don't let anyone steal your dreams.

Set long term mid term and short term goals. Your daily list will keep you on track.
If you don't know where you're going you are never going to get there.

When you know where you are going your brain goes into "HOW" mode. And if you get lost - wind down the window and ask for directions (Advice)

Set SMART goals: Specific Measurable Actionable Realistic and a Time to start and finish. It is important to write goals down!

If you always do what you've always done - you'll always get what you've always got!

If you want a different outcome change your approach. As it takes 21 days for a human being to develop new habits try a new behavior for 21 days and you can do it for life.

Phone your customers early - at 8.30 am before they go into meetings.

Ask a hundred customers "What's the one thing we can do better next time"? And do them.

Cosset your customer: Eye contact, cheery hello and greet them by name, mirror their body language.

If you think you know what your customers want - you're in trouble - ask them what they want. You have two ears and one mouth use them in that proportion.

When you are with customers take the cotton wool out of your ears and put it in your mouth.

Think of sales as an inverted triangle 20 letters get me10 fact-finding visits, which in turn get four proposals, which get me on average 2 new sales. (See page 59)

Always ask "Did you find everything you were looking for in the store today?" - If the answer is "no" offer to order some if they want to become a regular customer...

More final thoughts...

For greater customer penetration: Draw a matrix: List customers down the left and products across the top. Who buys what? Fill in the intersecting squares. The blank squares are your "windows of opportunity" to sell other products in your range to existing customers...

Get on a sales course today. Like other technologies Sales technology changes every 12 months.

Turnover is vanity profit is sanity and cash is reality.

Keep prices in the upper quartile except those prices your customers are familiar with. (KVIs) keep those lower than the competition.

Split your work into maintenance (mowing the lawn) and progression (paving the lawn) make time for progression jobs every day.

Put the wall planner up as early as possible at least August for next year. Book holidays and days off first in permanent ink. If you want four holidays a year, book the tickets and you'll find the money and the time.

If you want to be rich lock away 15% of your wages in a high yield account before you get your hands on it. Invest it at compound interest.

Do the books yourself. Use pie charts to "see" where your money goes

Stop doing work and start building a business.

Entrepreneurs don't work in a business they work on the business. Build a business that works when you don't.

Use operating manuals and organisation charts for staff consistency.

…And of course… **Good Luck!**

See: www.tomedge.co.uk for lots of free help and 101 free Hot Tips

Now print off page 89 to see if we can help you further with low cost e-books and audio programmes:

----- **CUT THIS FORM OUT** ----

Tom Edge
Training Projects
6, Himley Crescent
Wolverhampton
WV4 - 5DA England
email: tom@Over50.Biz
web site: www.Over50.Biz

Make cheques payable to: Training Projects

ORDER FORM

Your post Code:
House number:

INVOICE NO: 216854

ORDER DATE:

Send To: (BLOCK CAPITALS}

Post Code   House Number:

TICK √	YOUR CHEQUE NUMBER	DATE	DATE POSTED	TERMS SENT
Book or CD or Tape				

QTY	DESCRIPTION	UNIT PRICE	AMOUNT
	Over50.Biz age is no barrier Printed Book, or e-book on (CD)	£ 20.00	
	Selling For The Over 50's e-book (CD)	£ 20.00	
	12 ways to give your business the edge Audio (CD or Tape)	£ 20.00	
	How to beat a recession and speed your recovery Audio (CD)	£ 20.00	
	How to give Unforgettable Customer Service e-book (CD)	£ 20.00	
	How to Market, Advertise and Promote Your Business e-book (CD)	£ 20.00	
		SUBTOTAL	
	Postage & Packing (Add £1.50 for CDs and tapes)		
		TOTAL DUE	

Make all cheques/money orders payable to: Training Projects
No fuss unconditional guarantee

Payment to: Training Projects, 6, Himley Crescent, Wolverhampton WV4 - 5DA with this form.

If you have any questions concerning this invoice or the products, call: 01902-335507

Thank You For Your Business

Have you visited **www.tomedge.co.uk** for 101 Free Hot Tips yet?

Tom Edge Seminars and Workshops

For more details and Tom's availability please call Tom direct on 01902 335507